CW01020846

Contents

Thank you very much for buying this book.

I hope you will enjoy cooking these recipes as much as I enjoyed writing this little book.

In the first chapter, you will find simple, vegan recipes with prep time, directions, nutritional facts.

Then we will talk about my recipe philosophy.

And in the last chapter, I will introduce to you my cooking ideas.

Happy reading and Bon appetite!

Chapter 1: Simple Vegan Recipes

∞∞∞

Breakfast Recipes

∞∞∞

Apple Oatmeal

Prep time: 5 minutes ~ Cooking time: 20 minutes ~ Servings: 2

Ingredients

1 cup cut oats
2 teaspoon coconut oil
1 cup apples, chopped
2 ½ cup water
3 tablespoon brown sugar
1 teaspoon vanilla extract
½ teaspoon ground cinnamon

Directions

1. Press the Sauté mode on your instant pot.
2. Place the coconut oil, apples, brown sugar, vanilla extract, and ground cinnamon in the instant pot. (If you don't have an instant pot, you can cook it as normal)
3. Add cut oats and stir.
4. Sauté the mixture for 4-5 minutes. Stir it from time to time.
5. Then add water and mix it up.
6. Close the lid and press Manual mode (High pressure).
7. Cook the oatmeal for 13 minutes on High.
8. Then make quick pressure release.
9. Mix up the meal well before serving.

You can decorate your oatmeal with fruit, nuts, seeds of your choice.

Nutrition value/serving: calories 236, fat 6.2, fiber 5, carbs 42.9, protein 6.2

Savory Chickpea Omelet

Prep Time: 10 Minutes ~ Cook Time: 25-30 Minutes ~ Servings: 12

Ingredients

Olive oil, for preparing the muffin tin
2 cups chickpea flour
1 teaspoon salt
1 teaspoon baking powder (optional —makes them fluffier)
2 ½ cups water
1 tablespoon nutritional yeast (optional)
1 teaspoon dried herbs (optional)
½ teaspoon smoked paprika (optional) teaspoon garlic powder (optional)
½ teaspoon onion powder (optional)
2 cups chopped vegetables, such as zucchini, carrot, bell pepper, mushrooms, onion, com, peas, and olives
1 cup chopped spinach or kale (stems removed)

Directions

1. Preheat the oven to 400°F. Coat a muffin tin with

olive oil, line with paper muffin cups, or use a non-stick tin.

2. In a large bowl, combine the chickpea flour, salt, and baking powder (if using). Add the water and stir thoroughly to combine. You don't want any chunks of chickpea flour. The batter will be fairly runny. If using any optional seasonings, add them here and stir to combine.

3. Stir the veggies and spinach into the batter. Scoop the batter into the prepared tin, about 1/3 cup for each muffin. Bake for 25 to 30 minutes, until lightly browned on top. If you prefer them slightly gooey on the inside, take them out of the oven after 25 minutes; if you like them firmer, keep them in for 30 minutes.

4. Let cool for 10 minutes. Run a dinner knife around the inside of each cup to loosen, then tilt the cups on their sides in the muffin wells, so air gets underneath. These keep in an airtight container in the refrigerator for about five days or in the freezer indefinitely—thaw before reheating.

Nutritional facts: Calories: 66; Protein: 4g; Total fat: 1g; Saturated fat: Og; Carbohydrates: 10g; Fiber: 2g

Zucchini-Potato Hash Browns

Prep Time: 10 Minutes ~ Cooking Time:
25-30 Minutes ~ Servings: 4

Ingredients

1 potato, scrubbed or peeled and grated
½ zucchini, grated
2 tablespoons all-purpose flour
Salt to taste, divided
Freshly ground black pepper
1 scallion, chopped, or 1 teaspoon onion powder
(optional)
1 to 2 teaspoons olive oil
Salt

Directions

1. In a large bowl, combine the grated potato and zucchini. Sprinkle with salt and toss to combine. Push the vegetables to one side of the bowl and squeeze them to drain off some of the moisture, tipping the bowl to drain into the sink.

2. Add the flour, a pinch each of salt and pepper, and the scallion (if using), and toss to mix.

3. Place a large skillet over medium-high heat. While it heats, form the zucchini-potato mixture into 4 balls in the bowl.

4. Add the olive oil to the skillet and flatten the balls into the oiled pan. Cook for 5 to 7 minutes, until lightly browned on one side.

5. Flip and cook the other side until lightly browned.

Nutritional facts: Calories: 78; Protein: 2g; Total fat: 2g; Saturated fat: Og; Carbohydrates: 14g; Fiber: 2g

Main Dishes

∞∞∞

Vegan Hamburger

Great news! You can still eat a burger even as a vegan! Simply swap the beefburger for a plant-based option and cheese for a vegan cheese. You have two options - you can go to your local store and pick up a vegan burger from a freezer, or you can make your own. In case you decide to make your own, here is a recipe from tasty.co, which is one of my favorite websites when it comes to food (Tasty Vegan).

Prep time: 30 minutes ~ Cooking time: 20 minutes ~ Servings: 4

Ingredients

1 cup walnuts (100 g)
8 oz cremini mushroom (225 g)

2 tablespoons olive oil, divided
2 tablespoons low sodium soy sauce
½ teaspoon cumin
1 yellow onion, diced
2 cloves garlic, minced
1 teaspoon salt
½ teaspoon red bell pepper
1 tablespoon tomato paste
1 cup black beans (170 g), cooked
3 tablespoons beet, grated
1 cup brown rice (230 g), cooked
1 tablespoon vegan mayonnaise
1 teaspoon vegan Worcestershire
1 teaspoon liquid smoke
½ cup vital wheat gluten (6 5 g)
Vegan BBQ sauce, for basting
4 slices vegan cheese
4 burger buns
Vegan mayonnaise, to serve
Lettuce, to serve
Sliced tomato, to serve
Red onion, sliced, to serve

Directions

1. Add walnuts to the bowl of a food processor and pulse until crumbly. Add mushrooms and blend until finely chopped.
2. In a large skillet over medium heat, add 1 table-spoon olive oil and add the mushroom walnut mix-

ture, cooking for 5-8 minutes or until all moisture has evaporated.

3. Add soy sauce and cumin and cook, occasionally stirring, until dry. Transfer mixture to a bowl. 4. Add 1 tablespoon of olive oil to skillet.

5. Add the onion and cook, occasionally stirring, until semi-translucent, about 3 minutes.

6. Add garlic, salt, pepper, and tomato paste and cook for another 3-5 minutes until fragrant. Set aside.

7. Add black beans and onion mixture to food processor, and blend until mostly smooth.

8. Transfer mixture to bowl and add beets, rice, vegan mayo, Worcestershire sauce, and liquid smoke and stir until combined.

9. Add in vital wheat gluten and use hands to knead burger mixture together until all wheat gluten is fully incorporated.

10. Form burgers into 4 patties about 3-inches (7 cm) in diameter and 1-inch (2 cm) thick.

11. In a large cast-iron pan, over medium-high heat cooks patties about 5 minutes on each side.

12. Add on vegan cheese slices and melt. Assemble burger with vegan mayo, lettuce, tomato, and red onion.

Lentil Lasagna

Prep Time: 15 Minutes ~ Cook Time: 50 Minutes ~ Servings: 1

Ingredients

1 tbsp of olive oil
1 onion (chopped)
1 celery (chopped, stick)
1 carrot (chopped)
1 clove of garlic (crushed)
1 tbsp of com flour
2 cans of 400g lentils (drained, rinsed)
400g of tomato (chopped)
1 tsp of ketchup (mushroom)
1 tsp of vegetable stock (powder)
1 tsp of oregano (chopped)
2 cauliflower (heads, cut into florets and steamed)
2 tbsp of soya milk (unsweetened)

A pinch of grated nutmeg (freshly)
egg-free lasagna sheets (dried)

Directions

1. In a medium saucepan, heat the olive oil and sauté the onion, celery and carrot until softened, 5 minutes. Add the garlic, cook for 2 more minutes, and stir in the com flour and lentils.
2. Pour tomatoes, mushroom ketchup, stock powder, oregano and some seasoning. Bring to a boil for 15 minutes.
3. In a blender, process the cauliflower, soya milk, and nutmeg until smooth.
4. Preheat the oven to 350 F.
5. Layover the base, a ceramic casserole dish, a third of the lentil mixture then fill with a single layer of lasagna sheet. Top with another third of the lentil mixture, then spread over a third of the cauliflower purée, followed by a pasta layer. Finish with the last third of lentils and lasagna, then the remainder of the purée.
6. Cover with foil and bake for 35 to 45 minutes.
7. Remove the dish, foil, and allow cooling for 2 minutes.
8. Serve warm.

Instead of lentils, why don't you try "fake beef"?

Nutritional facts: Calories: 478; Fat: 27.7g; Saturated fat: 7.2g; Carbohydrate: 32g; Fiber: llg; Sugar: 13g; Protein: 29g; Iron: 4mg; Sodium: 604mg

Noodles with Sticky Tofu

Prep Time: 15 Minutes ~ Cook Time: 20 Minutes ~ Servings: 2

Ingredients

1/2 large size cucumber
2 tbsp of pure date sugar
100ml of wine vinegar (rice)
100ml of olive oil
200g pack of tofu (fir, cut into cubes)
2 tbsp of maple syrup
4 tbsp of white miso paste
30g of sesame seeds (white)
250g soba noodles (dried)
2 spring onions, (shredded, garnish)

Directions

1. Cut thin ribbons off the cucumber using a peeler, leaving behind the seeds. In a tub, place the ribbons and reserve. Heat the date sugar. Va tsp salt, 100 ml of water, and vinegar gently in a casserole over medium heat for 3 to 5 minutes until the date sugar is dissolved, then pour over the cucumbers and leave to pickle in the fridge while preparing the tofu.

2. In a large, nonstick frying pan, warm all but 1 tbsp of the oil over medium heat until bubbles start to come to the surface. Add the tofu and fry for 7-10 minutes until the tofu is uniformly golden brown, turning halfway. Remove the tofu from the pan and place on paper to drain grease.

3. Whisk together the pure maple syrup and miso in a small bowl. Place the sesame seeds on a plate.

4. Brush the tofu with the sticky pure maple syrup sauce and sprinkle with the sesame seeds.

5. Warm the noodles as instructed by the box, then drain and rinse under cold water.

6. Return the frying pan to heat with a little oil, throw in the noodles, and toss.

7. In 4 medium bowls, divide the noodles, tofu, pickled cucumber, spring onion, and some of the miso sauce.

8. Serve immediately.

Nutritional value/servings: Calories: 579; Fat: 20.5g; Saturated fat: 3.5g; Carbohydrate: 77g; Fiber 4g; Sugar 14g; Protein: 21 g; Iron: 4mg; Sodium:

688mg

Southwestern Stuffed Peppers

Prep Time: 30 Minutes ~ Cook Time: 1 Hour 20 Minutes ~ Servings: 4

Ingredients

½ cup low-sodium vegetable broth or 2 teaspoons
extra-virgin olive oil for sauteing
1 cup chopped onion
3 garlic cloves, chopped
1 cup uncooked wild rice
I ½ cups water
4 large red or yellow bell peppers
1 cup frozen com, thawed
1 cup cooked black beans
1/2 teaspoon salt
Freshly ground black pepper
1 (14.5-ounce) can diced tomatoes

green chilis, divided

Directions

1. Preheat the oven to 375 °F.
2. In a medium saucepan over medium heat, heat the broth or oil for sauteing. Add the onion and cook until soft and translucent, 4 to 5 minutes. Add the garlic and cook 1 minute more.
3. Add the rice and water. Bring to a boil, then cover and simmer for 30 minutes or until the rice is al dente, adding more water if needed.
4. Prepare the bell peppers by cutting off the tops and scooping out the seeds and as much of the membranes as you can. Set aside.
5. Put the cooked rice in a large bowl. Add the com, black beans, salt, pepper, and 1 ½ cups of the diced tomatoes and combine.
6. In the bottom of a medium baking dish, spread the remaining tomatoes. Stand up the peppers in the baking dish and fill them with the rice mixture. Put the tops back on.
7. Cover with foil and bake for 40 minutes. Remove the foil and bake for another 10 minutes.

Nutritional facts: Calories: 308; Fat: 2g; Saturated fat: 0g; Carbohydrate: 65g; Fiber: 11g; Sugar: 13g; Protein: 14g; Iron: 4mg; Sodium: 523mg

Lentil Gumbo

Prep time: 10 minutes ~ Cooking time: 23 minutes ~ Servings: 4

Ingredients

½ tablespoon garlic, diced
½ tablespoon coconut oil
1 bell pepper, chopped
1 celery stalk, chopped
½ teaspoon thyme
teaspoon coriander
1 teaspoon Cajun spices
½ teaspoon white pepper
½ cup lentils
1 ½ cup water

25

½ cup okra, chopped
1/2 cup tomatoes, diced, canned
1 teaspoon lemon juice
1 oz cauliflower, chopped
1 teaspoon salt

Directions

1. Preheat instant pot on Sauté mode and toss coconut oil inside.
2. Melt it and add bell pepper, garlic, celery stalk, thyme, coriander, and Cajun spices.
3. Mix up the mixture and cook for 10 minutes.
4. Then add all the remaining ingredients except salt.
5. Close and seal the lid.
6. Set Manual mode (high pressure) and cook gumbo for 13 minutes.
7. Then make quick pressure release.
8. Open the lid, add salt, and mix up the meal well.

If you don't have an instant pot, you can cook in your standard pot.

Nutrition value/serving: Calories 129, Fat 2.2, Fiber 9.3, Carbs 20.7, Protein 7.7

Simple Curried Vegetable Rice

Prep Time: 30 Minutes ~ Cooking Time:
10 Minutes ~ Servings: 4

Ingredients

2 cups chopped Carrots
1 cup chopped spinach
2 tsp ginger
1 medium broccoli, chopped
Salt to taste
1 cup cooked Brown Rice
2 cloves garlic, minced
Pepper (to taste)
1 tsp curry Powder

Directions

1. Before you begin cooking, you will want to take some prep time to chop up all of your vegetables beforehand. When they are cut into smaller pieces, this means they will cook faster!

2. Once your ingredients are prepared, take out a pan and begin to heat it over a medium heat. Once warm, add in some olive oil and then sprinkle in the garlic and the gin-

3. Next, you will want to add in the broccoli and carrots. At this point, season with salt and pepper and cook for two minutes.

4. Once the vegetables are cooked to your liking, add in the cooked brown rice along with the curry powder and toss the ingredients until everything is well coated.

5. Finally, add in the spinach and cook for another minute or until it becomes wilted. Season with some more salt and pepper, and then your meal will be ready just like that!

Nutritional facts: Calories: 280 Proteins: 10gCarbs: 50g Fats: 5g

Jen's Cannellini Meatballs with Sun-dried Tomatoes

Prep Time: 20 Minutes ~ Cook Time: 30 Minutes ~ Servings: 4

Ingredients

1/3 cup low-sodium vegetable broth or 2 teaspoons
extra-virgin olive oil for sautéing
1/2 cup chopped onion
3 garlic cloves, chopped
1 cup canned cannellini beans, drained
and rinsed, aquafaba liquid
1 cup cooked farro
1/4 cup chopped fresh basil, or more
sun-dried tomatoes in oil, drained and coarsely

chopped
1/2 teaspoon salt
Freshly ground black pepper
1/2 cup breadcrumbs

Directions

1. Preheat the oven to 375°F. Line a large baking sheet with parchment paper.
2. In a medium sauté pan over medium heat, heat the broth or oil for sauteing. Add the onion and sauté until soft and translucent, 4 to 5 minutes. Add the garlic and cook for another minute.
3. Add the cannellini beans, 2 tablespoons of the aquafaba, farro, basil, onion-garlic mixture, tomatoes, salt, and pepper to a food processor. Pulse a few times until combined. Add the breadcrumbs and pulse a few more times. (I like it to have a little texture.) Taste and adjust the seasoning if needed. Add another tablespoon aquafaba if you need it to bind more.
4. Scoop out about 2 tablespoons of the mixture and gently form a small ball about 1 1/2 inches in diameter.
5. Place on the baking sheet. Repeat until you have used up the mixture. You will have 10 to 12 meatballs.
6. Bake for 25 minutes, until browned and firm.

Nutritional facts: Calories: 223; Fat: 4g; Saturated fat: 0g; Carbohydrate: 25g; Fiber: 6g; Sugar: 2g; Protein: 9g; Iron: 3mg; Sodium: 387mg

Lentil Steak

Prep time: 10 minutes ~ Cooking time: 8 minutes ~ Servings: 2

Ingredients

1 cup lentils, cooked
1/2 cup bread crumbs
3 tablespoons wheat flour
1 teaspoon salt
1/2 teaspoon chili pepper
1 teaspoon dried oregano
1 tablespoon olive oil

Directions

1. Place lentils into the mixing bowl and mash them with the help of the fork.
2. After this, add wheat flour, salt, chili pepper, and dried oregano.
3. Mix up the mixture until homogenous.
4. With the help of the fingertips, make 2 balls and press them to make steak shape.
5. Preheat instant pot on sauté mode.
6. Then add olive oil.
7. Coat lentil steaks in bread crumbs.

8. Put the steaks in the preheated olive oil.
9. Cook them for 3 minutes from each side or until they are light brown.

Nutrition value/serving: Calories 551, fat 9.7, fiber 31.2, carbs 86.7, protein 29.7

Soups

∞∞∞

Spinach and Broccoli Soup

Prep time: 10 minutes ~ Cooking time: 20 minutes ~ Servings: 4

Ingredients

3 shallots, chopped
1 tablespoon olive oil
2 garlic cloves, minced
1/2 pound broccoli florets
1/2 pound baby spinach
salt and black pepper to the taste
3 cups veggie stock
1 teaspoon turmeric powder
1 tablespoon lime juice

Directions

1. Heat up a pot with the oil over medium-high heat, add the shallots and the garlic and sauté for 5 minutes.
2. Add the broccoli, spinach, and the other ingredients, toss, bring to a simmer and cook over medium heat for 15 minutes.
3. Ladle into soup bowls and serve.

Nutritional facts: Calories 150, fat 3, fiber 1, carbs 3, protein 7

Zucchini and Cauliflower Soup

Prep time: 10 minutes ~ Cooking time: 25 minutes ~ Servings: 4

Ingredients

4 scallions, chopped
1 teaspoon ginger, grated
2 tablespoons olive oil
1-pound zucchinis, sliced
2 cups cauliflower florets
salt and black pepper to the taste
2 cups veggie stock
1 garlic clove, minced
1 tablespoon lemon juice
1 cup coconut cream

Directions

1. Heat up a pot with the oil over medium heat, add the scallions, ginger, and the garlic and sauté for 5 minutes.
2. Add the rest of the ingredients, bring to a simmer and cook over medium heat for 20 minutes.
3. Blend everything using an immersion blender, ladle into soup bowls and serve.

Nutritional facts: calories 154, fat 12, fiber 3, carbs 5, protein 4

Double-Garlic Bean and Vegetable Soup

Prep Time: 25 Minutes ~ Cooking time: 10 Minutes ~ Servings: 4

Ingredients

1 tablespoon olive oil
1 teaspoon fine sea salt
1 minced onion
5 cloves garlic, minced
2 cups chopped red potatoes
2/3 cup sliced carrots
1 teaspoon Italian seasoning blend
4 cups water, divided

1 can crushed tomatoes or tomato puree
1 head roasted garlic
2 tablespoons prepared vegan pesto,
plus more for garnish
15 oz. of white beans, drained and rinsed
1-inch (2.5 cm) pieces green beans
salt and pepper

Directions

1. Heat the oil and salt in a large soup pot over medium heat. Add the onion, garlic, potatoes, carrots, and celery. Cook for 4 to 6 minutes, occasionally stirring, until the onions are translucent. Add the seasoning blend, red pepper flakes, and celery seed and stir for 2 minutes. Add 3 cups (705 ml) of the water and the crushed tomatoes.
2. Combine the remaining 1 cup (235 ml) water and the roasted garlic in a blender. Process until smooth. Add to the soup mixture and bring to a boil. Reduce the heat to simmer and cook for 30 minutes.
3. Stir in the pesto, beans, and green beans. Simmer for 15 minutes. Taste and adjust the seasonings.
4. Serve each bowl with a dollop of pesto, if desired.

Nutritional facts: Calories 140, Fat 7, Fiber 14, Carbs 4, Protein 21

Tuscan White Bean Soup

Prep Time: 10 Minutes ~ Cooking tine: 15 Minutes ~ Servings: 4

Ingredients

1 to 2 teaspoons olive oil
1 onion, chopped
4 garlic cloves, minced, or 1 teaspoon garlic powder
2 carrots, peeled and chopped
1 tablespoon dried herbs
Pinch freshly ground black pepper
Pinch red pepper flakes
4 cups vegetable Broth or water
2 (15-ounce) cans white beans, such as cannellini,
navy, or great northern, drained and rinsed
2 tablespoons freshly squeezed lemon juice
2 cups chopped greens, such as spinach, kale,
arugula, or chard
salt

Directions

1. Heat the olive oil in a large soup pot over medium-high heat. Add the onion, garlic (if using fresh), carrots, and a pinch of salt. Sauté for about 5 minutes, occasionally stirring, until the vegetables

are lightly browned. Sprinkle in the dried herbs (plus the garlic powder, if using), black pepper, and red pepper flakes and toss to combine.

2. Add the vegetable broth, beans, and another pinch of salt and bring the soup to a low simmer to heat through. If you like, make the broth a bit creamier by puréeing 1 to 2 cups of soup in a countertop blender and returning it to the pot. Alternatively, use a hand blender to purée about one-fourth of the beans in the pot.

3. Stir in the lemon juice and greens, and let the greens wilt into the soup before

 serving. Leftovers will keep in an airtight container for up to 1 week in the refrigerator or up to 1 month in the freezer.

Nutritional facts: Calories: 14 5; Protein: 7g; Total fat: 2g; Saturated fat: Og; Carbohydrates: 26g; Fiber: 6g

Desserts

∞∞∞

Peach Sorbet

Prep Time: 15 Minutes ~ Cooking Time: 0 Minutes ~ Servings: 4

Ingredients

5 peaches, peeled, pitted, and chopped
¾ cup sugar
Juice of 1 lemon or 1 tablespoon
prepared lemon juice

Directions

1. In the bowl of a food processor, combine all the ingredients and process until smooth.

2. Pour the mixture into a 9-by-1 3-inch glass pan. Cover tightly with plastic wrap. Freeze for 3 to 4 hours.

3. Remove from the freezer and scrape the sorbet into a food processor. Process until smooth. Freeze for another

Mixed Berries and Cream

Prep Time: 10 Minutes ~ Cooking Time: 0 Minutes ~ Servings: 4

Ingredients

two 15-ounce cans full-fat coconut milk
3 tablespoons agave
1/2 teaspoon vanilla extract
1 - pint fresh blueberries
2 - pints fresh raspberries
1 - pint fresh strawberries, sliced

Directions

1. Refrigerate the coconut milk overnight. When you

open the can, the liquid will have separated from the solids. Spoon out the solids and reserve the liquid for another purpose.

2. In a medium bowl, whisk the agave and vanilla extract into the coconut solids. Divide the berries among four bowls. Top with the coconut cream. Serve immediately.

Lime and Watermelon Granita

Prep Time: 15 Minutes ~ Chilling Time: 6 Minutes ~ Servings: 4

Ingredients

cups seedless watermelon chunks
juice of 2 limes or 2 tablespoons prepared lime juice
1/2 cup sugar
strips of lime zest, for garnish

Directions

1. In a blender or food processor, combine the watermelon, lime juice, and sugar and process until smooth. You may have to do this in two batches. After processing, stir well to combine both batches.
2. Pour the mixture into a 9-by-1 3-inch glass dish. Freeze for 2 to 3 hours.
3. Remove from the freezer and use a fork to scrape

the top layer of ice. Leave the shaved ice on top and return to the freezer. In another hour, remove from the freezer and repeat. Do this a few more times until all the ice is scraped up. Serve frozen, garnished with strips of lime zest.

Chocolate Pudding

Ingredients

1/3 cup sugar
1/3 cup unsweetened cocoa powder
3 cups unsweetened almond milk
1/4 cup cornstarch
pinch of sea salt
1 teaspoon vanilla extract

Directions

1. In a medium bowl, whisk together the sugar and cocoa powder to combine thoroughly. In a large saucepan over medium heat, whisk together the cocoa mixture and 2 1/2 cups of the almond milk. Bring to a boil, stirring constantly. Remove from the heat.

2. In a small bowl, whisk together the remaining 1/2 cup almond milk and cornstarch. Stir into the cocoa mixture and return to medium heat. Add the salt.

3. Stirring constantly, bring the pudding to a boil.

It will begin to thicken. Boil for 1 minute. Remove from the heat and stir in the vanilla. Chill before serving.

Chocolate Macaroons

Prep Time: 10 Minutes ~ Cooking Time: 15
Minutes ~ Makes 8 To 10 Macaroons

Ingredients

1 cup unsweetened shredded coconut
2 tablespoons cocoa powder
2/3 cup coconut milk
1/4 cup agave
pinch of sea salt

Directions

1. Preheat the oven to 350°F. Line a baking sheet
with parchment paper. In a medium saucepan, cook
all the ingredients over medium-high heat until a
firm dough is formed.
2. Scoop the dough into balls and place them on the
baking sheet. Bake for 15 minutes, remove from the
oven and let cool on the baking sheet.
3. Serve cooled macaroons or store in a tightly
sealed container for up to 1 week.

Coconut and Almond Truffles

Prep Time: 15 Minutes ~ Cooking Time: 0
Minutes ~ Makes 8-10 Truffles

Ingredients

1 cup pitted dates
1 cup almonds
1/2 cup sweetened cocoa powder, plus extra for
coating
1/2 cup unsweetened shredded coconut
1/4 cup pure maple syrup
1 teaspoon vanilla extract
1 teaspoon almond extract
1/4 teaspoon sea salt

Directions

1. In the bowl of a food processor, combine all the ingredients and process until smooth. Chill the mixture for about 1 hour.
2. Roll the mixture into balls and then roll the balls in cocoa powder to coat. Serve immediately or keep chilled until ready to serve.

Smoothies and Beverages

∞∞∞

Almond Chocolate Milk

Prep Time: 5 minutes ~ Servings: 1

Ingredients

2 ice cubes
1/2 tsp cinnamon
drops stevia sweetener
1 scoop protein powder, chocolate flavored
1/2 vanilla stick, crushed
1 1/2 cups almond milk, unsweetened
2 tbsp coconut oil

Directions

1. Take all of the ingredients, besides the ice, and add to the blender.

2. Blend them together for about a minute. If you are using the ice, add it in and blend for another half a minute.

3. Move the milk to a large cup and then serve with a bit more cinnamon on top.

Nutritional facts: Calories 422, Carbs 1.3g, Fat 34.8g, Protein 25.5g

Protein Espresso

Prep Time: 5 minutes ~ Servings: 1

Ingredients

2 tbsps coconut cream
1/2 tsp cinnamon
1 tbsp cocoa powder
1/2 cup boiled water
3/4 vanilla stick
A scoop of chocolate flavored soy protein
3 tsp coconut butter or oil
A cup freshly brewed espresso

Directions

1. Make sure that you are using fresh and hot espresso.

2. Add all of the ingredients that are above to a blender that is heat safe, along with the boiled water. If you want this to be iced, then use ice instead of the hot water.

3. Blend these ingredients together for about a minute before moving to a big coffee cup. Top with some of the coconut cream and stir around before enjoying.

Nutritional facts: Calories 441, Carbs 5.6g, Fat 34.8g, Protein 2 5.4g

Chapter 8: The Recipe Philosophy

"Let food be thy medicine, and medicine be thy food."— Hippocrates

I think it's important to teach you not how to follow recipes but actually teach you how to think as "a chef." Because each and every one of us is unique, is different, has different taste buds, and we just simply like different things. If I present you with 100 recipes, we can be absolutely sure that some of you will like them, and some of you will not.

I believe it's important to take each recipe as guidance and "play" with it - edit it. Be creative, add things – the spices you like that make your taste buds happy. There are thousands of cookbooks and recipes online. My approach is a little bit different. I offer ideas for simple and easy recipes that you can adapt to your desires.

I am very spoiled when it comes to taste; I need my dish to be very aromatic, full of flavor. I take a recipe and modify it to suit my taste. Spices are an amazing thing; you can take the same dish, and just with spices, you can turn it into something so wonderful.

You can add oregano, basil, paprika, chili, but for me, the winners are always garlic & onion. But again - not everybody likes it - so do it the way you like it! Add what you like - not what the recipe asks for. You will find my recipe to be a bit unorthodox! They're a little bit "free."

So in the next chapter you will find some "Ideas from Lucy's Kitchen".

Most of your favorite recipes that you are already cooking and love can be turned into plant-based options. Put simply - you just have to remove the meat, cheese, milk, etc. These days you will find a lot of alternatives in your supermarket, from tofu to fake meat.

My intention is not to provide you with hundreds of recipes, but just to give you ideas and show you that plant-based living is not as hard as it seems, it's not expensive, and it is also fun.

From my experience, the easiest way to cook is by watching cooking videos. I would recommend following vegans and people on a plant-based diet on Instagram as they give tips and make short videos of recipes. You can also find many recipes on YouTube and on the internet - but what am I saying? I am sure you know this already.

Chapter 9: Cooking Ideas From Lucy's Kitchen

∞∞∞

✲✲✲ Granola ✲✲✲

These days, there are a multitude of granola types that you can buy in the supermarket, even versions with reduced sugar, but it's still quite fun to make your own. There are plenty of recipes on the internet, but I always try to keep it simple. I simply heat two big spoons of coconut oil & maple syrup, pour this over oats, nuts, chia seeds - you can use anything you like - the fun thing about granola is that you can put anything you like in it! Seeds, nuts, dried fruit, coconut.

I love coconut in granola as it gives it natural sweetness!
Mix and bake it until it's golden brown.

My favorite way of eating it is with soy vanilla yogurt. Awesome!

*** Tacos ***

I used to love beef tacos with plenty of cheese and onion. We can still have them - just change beef for fake minced beef (you will find it in a freezer in your local store). Put a bit of olive oil on your pan, add this fake beef, then add lots of taco spice so the spice will cover each bit. Once cooked and dry, add a bit of vegan cheese, so it melts and stirs together.

Ingredients

Taco shells (you can even buy a taco kit from store)
1 Lettuce
Fake beef & cheese
1 onion
1 Pack of tomatoes
1 Taco spice - you will find it in spice section in the store

For salsa you can either buy one from the store or if you are onion lover and you have pulse blender check out my recipe:

You will need:
Salsa from store -1 glass can - Sweet and crunchy baby tomatoes - half pack or two big tomatoes (again sweet- that's the magic)
Onion-one big one
2 Cloves of garlic

To make salsa I would recommend to buy one salsa from store - any that you like and those sweet and crunchy baby tomatoes - cut them in half and cut the onion in quarters and one or two peeled garlic you can cut it in half, (some people add cilantro and lemon juice, but I prefer it without) add salt & pepper and pulse mix few times, so you create a chunky mixture. To this, you will add this normal -store-bought- salsa and viola - amazing crunchy full of flavor salsa can see the light of the day! Then just heat your taco shells, and the "beef" to them, on top put salsa, lettuce, and some vegan cheese, and you are ready to eat!

If you're in the mood for Mexican, but don't want tacos, why don't you try tortillas?

They're best served with plenty of bell peppers and onions, which you can fry in the pan with some tofu or tempeh. Add lots of fajita seasoning, some "fake cheese", lettuce and wrap it all up! Amazing, healthy, and so delicious!

*** Stir-Fry ***

Again, this is something that can be done in many ways; the good news is you can buy many different sauces in your store and then just cook as per instruction, I, for example, love Korean sauces, but popular are garlic sauce, sweet and sour, etc. I am sure you are familiar with all Asian sauces out there. You can check on the packaging, whether they are actually vegan or use the vegan app on your phone.

I sauté all veggies I can find in the fridge or in the shop. For this, I definitely recommend mushrooms, green beans, peppers, bok choy, and broccoli. On the side, make noodles or rice, then serve together, and don't forget spring onion at the end for extra flavor. I usually upgrade the sauce by adding soy sauce, fresh garlic, more spice.

You know me now, I am all about garlic.

*** Pasta ***

Pasta can be done in many ways, and most of the time, you keep cooking your favorite recipes, just remove meat, substitute or add veggies instead. My favorite is pasta with spinach, garlic, vegan cheese & soy cream. Sauté onion, garlic, maybe add some vegan ham, or zucchini and mushrooms, cook pasta as per instructions on a pack, then mix everything together, add spices such as oregano, garlic, paprika spice, a little bit of chili, add "cheese" or nutritional east & soy cream and all done. Nice and easy.

My second favorite recipe is when you cook pasta, sauté all veggies you can find -1 usually add zucchini, mushrooms, bell pepper, sun-dried tomatoes, leek, onion or spring onion, a little bit of eggplant, add a lot of sun-dried pesto, which you can buy in a shop in the section where are sauces, add basil, spices that you desire and all done!

*** 𝒟eans 𝒥uning ***

Baked beans from a can, half a cup of black beans, sweet- corn (frozen or from a can), spices such as: salt, pepper, paprika, garlic, parsley, you can add chili/cayenne pepper if you like it spicy- start with less, you can always add more later. You can add vegan cheese. Heat everything and serve alone or with a tortilla.

Put a tortilla on a pan and let it heat - you can have it soft, or if you leave it on a pan for a while, it will be a bit crispier.

*** Curry Zucchini ***

Ingredients
2 medium potatoes - cut in chunks
1 onion cut in chunks
2 cloves of garlic
1 big zucchini or two small cuts in chunks
1 carrot cut in chunks
curry powder
plant-based cream
vegetable stock
olive oil fry diced onion & garlic

Directions
First, fry diced onion for a little bit, then add garlic

and, in the meantime, boil water 0,5 L - put vegetable cube stock in a 0,5 L mug, add boiled water a
mix.
Add curry powder (start with less, maybe a teaspoon, and you will add later depends on your
taste) for a few seconds mix, then add the rest of the
vegetable. Pour over the stock. Simmer for about
10-20 mins - until vegetable is soft. Now, it is up to
you whether you want to take half and blend it in a
mixer and then put it back and stir to create more
creamy texture; blend it all; or you can leave it as it
is.

I usually leave it as is because once veggie is soft, I
stir and stir, and those potatoes & zucchini create
creamy mixture even without blending in a mixer.
At the end, add cream - up to you how much you
like.

And then you can play with spices; I sometimes add
more garlic powder, paprika powder, onion powder,
more curry powder, and a little bit of maple syrup.
Once you cook it, you can taste it and play with it
and see what works well.

✳✳✳ *Vegetable in Oven* ✳✳✳

This is a simple dish, and you can never go wrong with it. Just cut any vegetable you like, I make it with potatoes, peppers, tomatoes, zucchini, onion, carrot, asparagus, sweet potatoes - you can just add anything and then cut all in pieces, put it in a bowl, drizzle olive oil (for baking), add salt, pepper, any spices that you desire, parsley, garlic, rosemary, paprika, anything you like and bake until veggie is soft.

This also goes well with Soy/Garlic/Marple syrup or brown sugar Mushrooms. You can make them on a pan - put some oil, mushrooms cut in smaller or bigger pieces - up to you and add garlic (dry, fresh), a bit

of soy sauce and maple syrup or brown sugar. Wait
till it cooks, and most of the water is gone.

*** *Avocado Toast* ***

Famous avocado toast: the old vegan classic. It is simple. You can just mash the avocado, add little salt & pepper maybe even little lemon juice, or herbs mix and spread it over your favorite bread. On top, you can add tomatoes or roasted chickpeas -1 can of chickpeas (drain with a paper towel) mix with oil and spices of your liking and oven bake for 20-30 minutes - depends how crispy you like them.

Nut Butter Toast/ Tortilla

This is an old classic as well - there are many nut butters in your store - from peanut, almond, cashew, even those with cacao - hazelnut - my favorite. Just spread over your favorite bread. You can spread nut butter over the tortilla and put a banana inside and roll and cut - you will have little tortilla "sushi".

I would like to throw also a few ideas, for example: **Thai green or red curry** - a great option for vegans if you like a bit spicy meals. Simply more veggie and tofu instead of meat.

Broccoli is really good when you toss florets with lots of spices and oil and then bake for about 15 minutes and sprinkle over some vegan cheese.

A few years back I was obsessed with this **lovely broccoli soup**; it's really simple just take broccoli head, one leek, few potatoes and boil everything together in a pot - start with potatoes when they boil for 5 minutes add broccoli & leek and one or two cubes of vegetable stock. Cook everything, and once done, mix it in a blender for a creamy texture. Check the taste and then play with it by adding some salt & pepper (even garlic); and all done.

A simple snack is **hummus and carrots;** you can just buy it in a shop in a snack section or cut carrots and buy hummus alone.

✳✳ *Treats* ✳✳✳

If you fancy something frozen, there is a simple solution that you can make at home too! Of course, you can find many vegan ice creams at the store. But they are full of "bad sugar". If you'd like to try something a little bit healthier, opt for homemade frozen yogurt or frozen fruit! Always freeze your fruit first and only then blend them in your food processor.

If you fancy mango, mix it with some coconut milk, yogurt, and maple syrup. This one is actually really refreshing.

Other ideas include mixing frozen banana with peanut butter & yogurt.

While we're on the topic of bananas - try banana ice cream - mix a few frozen bananas with a bit of plant milk, peanut or almond butter, tbsp of cocoa powder (if you like it chocolate-yyy) and freeze. You can make this with some other fruit too. Vegans call it "nicecream".

✱✱✱ *Guilt-Free Bonbons* ✱✱✱

Instead of snacking on bonbons, why don't you just freeze some fruit - you can freeze blueberries or grapes and snack on them during the day - that's a great guilt-free alternative when you start craving something sugary. It tastes delightful.

Mango is also great; it just needs to be sweet and ripe.
You can basically freeze anything, just cut it into pieces.

*** Smoothies/Nicecream ***

There are many ways you can make a smoothie, and if you search online, you will find endless recipes not just from fruit, but from veggies as well.

What I like to use as my base for any smoothie I make is 100% pressed apple juice (or any other juice of your preference). I throw it into the mixer along with any fruit I can find in my freezer.

The most common fruits I use are frozen blueberries, strawberries, a bit of spinach, and a bit of apple juice - just enough to get a nice, creamy consistency.

Other times I throw peaches, some pineapple, a banana, and mango into the mixer, and this time
 I would use 100% squeezed orange juice as the

base.

I like to make smoothies with frozen banana and a bit of mango too, mixed with plant milk (coconut is especially good in this one). This makes for a lovely dessert.

You can also try just banana with plant milk and cocoa powder!

With smoothies, you can be creative as pretty much any fruit you have at home will taste great and will make a fantastic smoothie.

And to make it even healthier, just add hemp hearts or ground flax seeds or try adding different kinds of superfoods like spirulina and Chlorella to give it more vital nutrients.

Vegan protein powder is also another great option if you want to make your smoothie more nutritious.

One last thing...

We would love to hear your feedback about this book!

If you enjoyed this book or found it useful, we would be very grateful if you posted a short review on Amazon. Your support does make a difference, and we read every review personally.

If you would like to leave a review, all you need to do is click the review link on this book's page on Amazon. Thank you for your support!

Printed in Great Britain
by Amazon

50585442R00047